Frontispiece

Bath today is a vibrant, cosmopolitan and energetic place. Its world-class university, good transport links and fashionable shops, cafes and restaurants have all kept the city vibrant and popular. Combined with this, Bath's history, unique architecture and other magnificent visitor attractions all make Bath one of the UK's 'must see' destinations.

An important note to readers

Although every effort has been made to ensure the accuracy and correctness of the information contained in this book, it may change at any time for many reasons. The author shall not be responsible for any loss or damage experienced by readers resulting in errors in information or omissions from this book.

Creatspace Publishing

© 2015 by Trevor J. Price

All rights reserved

First edition 2015

About the author

Trevor is an English anglophile who adores writing, especially about stunningly beautiful places like the city of Bath.

This City Guide to Bath is the second in Trevor's popular 'City Guide to . . .' series which focuses upon a city that has a fond place in Trevor's heart and nostalgia. Having lived, worked and visited Bath, Trevor has spent much time enjoying its history, its stunning architectural beauty and its world class events and opportunities.

As well as writing, walking is another one of Trevor's passions, and one that is completely fulfilled when in Bath. Whatever sort of walker you are - whether you are aimlessly wandering around this World Heritage city, or you are more energetically exploring Bath's canal and riverside pathways and its extensive surrounding countryside rambles – Bath has something for you.

Trevor is a university academic and so writing is his love and drives him on. Combining an internationally-renowned jewel of a city with Trevor's skillfully crafted and useful descriptions provides you with a gem of a book that will help you to fully explore and enjoy all the treats that the city of Bath has to offer.

Book summary

With an eye for the things that really matter to travelers, Trevor loves to combine his passion for good photography with powerfully descriptive writing. In this way, Trevor's skillful writing takes his readers to places they haven't yet been and with his beautiful photography, Trevor also enables readers to see what these new and exciting places look like.

Throughout his travels Trevor has used many guide books to help him find his way. After a while, Trevor realized that what are missing are guide books that tell things like they really are, in a handy size and with a good balance of good quality photographs and descriptive text. This is exactly what he has put together in this City Guide to Bath.

This book is aimed at those who want a quick and easy-to-use guide that doesn't bore with long-winded details and lots of text about irrelevant and boring stuff. You'll find no 'blah-blah' here – only stuff that you really need to know to have a great time in and around Bath.

The city of Bath is an amazing place and so unique in the world. It's a city that has evolved over time in response to the political, social and economic conditions prevalent throughout its history, and which has created the distinctive character of Bath which is so attractive to the people who live here, as well as those who visit.

Bath is locally, nationally and internationally significance because (Bath and North East Somerset Local Authority 2005):

- The whole city has been a UNESCO World Heritage Site since December 1987

- Of the hot springs in the centre of the city

- Part of the city, which covers 3672 acres (1,486 hectares), is designated as a special conservation area

- The city sits within the Cotswolds Area of Outstanding Natural Beauty

- Within the city are around 5,000 buildings that are of special architectural or historic importance

- Of the city's five ancient monuments

- Of the nine historic landscapes within the city which are contained within the English Heritage Register of Historic Parks and Gardens

Contents

1. The Origins of the City 15
    - Before the Romans 17
    - The Roman city of Aquae Sulis 20
    - Richard 'Beau' Nash – a Bath hero! 25
    - Architectural highlights 29
    - 20th Century Bath 31

2. Travel to, from and within Bath 33
    - AIR 33
        - Bristol airport 33
        - Heathrow airport 34
        - Gatwick airport 34
    - RAIL 35
    - ROAD 35
        - Park and ride 36
        - Bicycle 36
        - Two Tunnels Greenway 37
        - Bus 37

3. Places of interest within the city 39
    - American Museum 39
    - Assembly Rooms 40
    - Bath Abbey 43
    - Bath Abbey Heritage Vaults Museum and Church yard 45
    - Bath Spa Railway Station 46
    - Bath Bus and Coach Station 48
    - Botanical Gardens 49
    - Green Park Station 49

	Guildhall	50
	Guildhall Market	51
	Herschel Museum of Astronomy	51
	Pulteney Bridge	52
	Pump Room	55
	Queens Square	58
	Roman Baths	59
	Royal Crescent	62
	Royal Victoria Park	64
	The Holbourne Museum and Sydney Gardens	65
	The Circus	66
	Theatre Royal	68
	Thermae Bath Spa	69
	Victoria Art Gallery	69
4	**Around Bath and further afield**	**71**
	Bristol	71
	Cardiff	72
	Kennet and Avon Canal	73
	London	75
	Oxford	76
	Stonehenge	77
	The Cotswolds	77
5	**Suggested itineraries**	**79**
	See all the sights	81
	Living history: A Roman and Georgian Jewel	85
	Parks and gardens - green, open spaces	87
	Museums – a look at times gone by	89
	Shopping	91

6 Works Cited 93

List of figures

Figure 1. The city of Bath's UNESCO World Heritage plaque which is located near the Pump Rooms...15

Figure 2. Bishop Oliver's dream-come-true as angelic figures climb up and down celestial ladders above the entrance to Bath Abbey 23

Figure 3. The Royal Crescent 28

Figure 4. The Tea Room, part of Bath's Assembly Rooms. 42

Figure 5. Pulteney Bridge 54

Figure 6. Entrances to the Pump Room and Roman Baths...................................56

1   THE ORIGINS OF THE CITY

Since 1987 the only complete English city to be classified a World Heritage Site, Bath straddles both sides of the River Avon in the south-west corner of Britain, just over 120 miles (190 km) by road, west from London. As its UNESCO plaque proclaims, (see Figure 1) Bath really is '. . . a masterpiece of human creative genius'.

Figure 1. The city of Bath's UNESCO World Heritage plaque which is located near the Pump Rooms.

According to its World Heritage Site inscription, Bath received its World Heritage Site status as (Smith 2010):

' . . . in spite of all the changes imposed upon it by the 20th century, Bath remains a beautiful city, set in a hollow *among hills and as architecturally exciting as it was in its Georgian heyday.'*

The UNESCO World Heritage List website (United Nations Education, Scientific and Cultural Organization 2015) explains that Bath is outstanding because of its

> *'Roman remains, especially the Temple of Sulis Minerva and the baths complex (based around the hot springs at the heart of the Roman town of Aquae Sulis, which have remained at the heart of the City's development ever since)* [which] *are amongst the most famous and important Roman remains north of the Alps, and marked the beginning of Bath's history as a spa town'.*

Bath and its residents had to wait a few hundred years after the Romans had left to experience its peak in popularity and economic prosperity. This high point in the city's history began when the Georgian mover-and-shaker, Richard Nash, also known as 'Beau' Nash, the nickname given to him by his aristocratic contemporaries, arrived in the city during 1705. Nash subsequently became instrumental in changing the face of this, then quite ordinary, place. Nash led the revolutionary changes in the city and soon became largely responsible for encouraging and enabling the development of Bath into a fashionable spa town popular with Georgian England's upper- and middle-classes. These relatively-wealthy people revelled in hob-knobbing with the aristocracy in Bath's then trendiest and most fashionable hot-spots, the Assembly Rooms and the Pump Room. These places, and others of the Georgian period, are still popular with visitors.

BEFORE THE ROMANS

Before the Romans arrived the countryside around the site of present-day Bath already had people living within it. For example, Neolithic and early Bronze Age tools made from flint and a Bronze Age burial mound suggest relatively large and well organized early settlements existed in the area (Bath and North East Somerset Local Authority 2005). Between the sixth and second centuries BC a hillfort at Little Solsbury was built near to the present-day village of Batheaston around 4 miles (6.4 km) north-east from Bath. As well as such defended hilltop sites, there would also have been a number of farmsteads on the more fertile lowland slopes; Sion Hill and Barrow Mead are just two examples where archeological remains of these have been recorded. What is a little curious however, is that nowhere within the area of the old walled city of Bath has any trace of pre-Roman occupation been found. This may be because the area was an inhospitable marshland of thick, black mud. Or it may have been that this was a sacred place surrounding the hot springs and so was revered by local people as something spiritually special and so not to be touched.

Legend has it that the father of King Lear, a Prince called Bladud, was the first to discover spring waters at the location of what is now the centre of the city in around 863 BC. Having spent time studying in Athens, Bladud had unfortunately caught leprosy, a mildly infectious disease that damages the small nerves on the victim's skin surface and which was quite prevalent at the time. This cruelly meant that even though he was a prince, with such a disease Bladud would not be allowed to inherit his father's throne as he had become an outcast. Fed-up with his predicament and the undoubted taunting and negative social stigma his disease would have caused, he decided to escape from the pressures of the Royal Court. So he decided to disguise himself as a swineherd (from the Old English word *'swynhyrde'* meaning a person who looks after pigs) and took a job tending a drove of pigs far away from the Palace and his father's Court. Bladud ended-up in the present day Avon Valley, and more precisely near to what is now the small town of Keynsham, which lies some 7.5 miles (12km) away from Bath westwards and on the way to Bristol.

As part of his job as a swineherd, Bladud had to seek food for the pigs that he was tending. A common food for pigs at the time was acorns and luckily for Bladud a plentiful, natural supply of acorns lay in a wood across the River Avon from where he kept the pigs. This meant that Bladud had to drive his pigs across the river at a ford shallow enough for his pigs to cross and which is now known as Swineford, before moving along the river hunting for food for the pigs.

Swineherds at that time lived and worked very close to their animals and it wasn't long before the pigs had also caught leprosy from Bladud. At places along the river, the pigs often wallowed in the warm, muddy water which had sprung out the ground. Bladud soon realised that after covering themselves in the muddy river water his pigs had eventually been cured of their leprosy. So with nothing to lose he too bathed in the warm mud and to his great relief he too eventually became cured. Now rid of his leprosy Bladud was once again welcomed back to the King's palace where he was restored to his position as heir to the throne.

As a way of giving thanks for becoming cured of leprosy, Bladud dedicated the area where he discovered the mud and its restorative powers to the Celtic goddess Sul. This legend and the apparent restorative powers of the naturally hot spring waters were influential spiritual signs to the indigenous Celtic people whose beliefs were based within nature and the countryside around them. As such the hot springs became a spiritually special place.

The Roman city of Aquae Sulis

After invading Britain, the Romans soon discovered the site of the hot springs in around 63AD and were quick to spot their beneficial potential and develop the area. The Romans hugely valued the health and personal hygiene benefits that natural hot springs and spas could provide. Roman engineers were able to harness the natural spa resources they found at Bath, soon deploying their technology to create a world-class destination resort for Roman dignitaries and other important people. As more and more Romans and others began settling in the area, a town developed which they named *Aquae Sulis* (when translated from the Roman Latin means *The waters of Sul*, in English*)*, as a tribute to the Celtic goddess Sul who was worshipped by the local indigenous population. But also due to its naturally hot, healing mineral spring waters, the Romans believed that the place had a strong connection to Minerva who was their own goddess of healing. So the Roman's decided to build a temple to both the Celtic Sul and the Roman Minerva deities at the site of the hot spring in Bath, locating them next to each other. The Gorgon's head from the pediment of the Temple of Sulis Minerva is an iconic representation of a mix of both the Roman and Celtic goddesses and is still used today; for example on the University of Bath's website at www.bath.ac.uk. The Romans therefore were responsible for developing Bath into what became an internationally famous spa retreat to where people from all over the Roman Empire would travel to bathe in what they believed to be its healing hot spring water. This heritage is reflected in modern Bath. For example Bath Spa is the name of the railway station.

In developing the hot springs the Romans used some impressive engineering structures. Some of these still exist and can still be seen at the Roman Baths. For example, a lead-lined reservoir which collects 240,000 gallons (1 million litres) of hot spring water which gurgles from the ground every day at an average temperature of about 115°F (45°C). Although the Roman Baths were left untended when the Romans left Britain, the Great Bath itself can still also be seen intact. It too is lined with lead and was designed with built-in seats for bathers to sit on whilst they dipped themselves in the green-tinged steaming-hot spring water. In its heyday the Roman complex also included a warm, wet room (which the Romans in Latin called a *tepidarium*), a hot, wet room (in Latin, a *caldarium*) and a hot, dry room (*laconium*) and which provided a social focus for the people of the town for almost 300 years.

The Romans left Bath in about 400AD. Even so, the city managed to retain its importance. For example in 973AD King Edgar of Wessex was crowned the first king of a unified England in Bath Abbey. This was quite a monumental time for England as before this the country had had been divided and ruled by several tribes, often wastefully and violently clashing with each other over needed resources. King Edgar's coronation was held in the then recently built Bath Abbey, which was constructed on the site of a church that had been built during 757AD. This church had been part of a Benedictine Monastery and was constructed using some of the masonry from the former Roman city. The coronation ceremony, devised by Saint Dunstan, the then Archbishop of Canterbury, is still used as the basis of British royal coronations.

Later in the 11th century when the Normans had seized power over England the Abbey was turned into a cathedral and dedicated to the Saints Peter and Paul. As time passed, the Abbey fell increasingly into disrepair. However during the 1490s, the then Bishop of Bath Oliver King, who had been appointed in 1495, had a dream in which he saw angels ascending and descending a ladder connecting heaven to earth. Taking it as a prophetic sign, the Bishop led the restoration of the Abbey and had angelic figures climbing up and down celestial ladders made from stone carved into the sides of the west face of the Abbey. See Figure 2. Eagle-eyed visitors may also spot the winding olive trees and a king's coronet carved out of stone around the Abbey entrance. Along with the busy angles, these icons are part of the visual 'signature' of Bishop Oliver King.

Figure 2. Bishop Oliver's dream-come-true as angelic figures climb up and down celestial ladders above the entrance to Bath Abbey

Queen Elizabeth I ruled England from 1558 to 1603 and in 1590 made Bath a city by granting it a Royal Charter. This was a huge boost to the place and meant that the Mayor and citizens of the new city were free to govern themselves and that (Mayor of Bath 2015):

- The Mayor and citizens have Aldermen and a Common Council. Derived from the old English 'ealdorman', Aldermen were traditionally 'older men' picked from the community to help run the local government.

- The Mayor is chosen yearly on the Monday before the Feast of St Michael, which happens on 29th September and which signals the start of autumn. However, back in Queen Elizabeth I's day this was a day of 'obligation', i.e. a rest day from work in order to allow people to attend mass.

- The Mayor, Aldermen and citizens retain the Council House within the Guildhall in which they hold the Council.

- Powers are granted to impose by-laws and to impose fines.

- The boundaries of the city were defined, with power to break through fences, buildings and enclosures.

- Powers were granted to make inhabitants free citizens or burgesses. A Burgess being a person having the right to be protected within the city in times of attack.

- Powers were granted to establish a prison and gaol.

- The Mayor became clerk of the market.

- Two markets could be held every week on Wednesday and Saturday.

- No stranger who was not a Freeman could sell in the city without license from the Mayor, except in the market or fair.

- The Mayor was made the Coroner for the city.

- The Mayor, Aldermen and citizens own the Baths, waste-ground lands and tenements.

Establishing Bath as a city was a significant development hugely raising its profile and importance at home and abroad.

RICHARD 'BEAU' NASH – A BATH HERO!

Due in part to its city status, but more so as a place favoured by royalty and aristocracy, the city of Bath continued to grow in popularity. In 1702-3 Queen Anne gave a further boost to Bath's prosperity when she visited this still most fashionable English spa resort. Of course with the Queen came her court and followers – most notably the Master of Ceremonies, a Welshman and dandy, Richard 'Beau' Nash. In Georgian days, the Master of Ceremonies would arrange a lot of society's important social life - events such as balls, dances and other social gatherings. He would choose who was invited, be chaperone to unaccompanied women, and would also ensure the smooth running of the entertainment. This was a very influential position and Beau soon got to know Bath society's key decision makers and other important people. Beau was also a person to get to know if you wanted to be included in the important social calendar. He could influence which parties, dances or balls you were, or were not, invited to. This had an important knock-on effect as it affected people's ability to network with influential dignitaries and contemporary decision-makers and so influenced social and professional success.

Beau had moved to Bath in 1705 and had become promoted from Assistant to full Master of Ceremonies when his boss was killed in a sword-fighting duel. This was a great opportunity for Beau. He was now very influential and laid down a set of rules for Bath society to follow. He started-off by banning the wearing of swords which swiftly put a stop to sword-fighting duels which were a violent but common way for gentlemen of the time to settle disputes. He also introduced a new code of conduct within society – which in turn affected people's behavior. He even set trends in fashion. For example he disliked wearing calf-length boots which were popular at the time, much preferring to wear shoes. Shoes then quickly became the rage with society figures and especially those who enjoyed ballroom dancing. They were, after all, much cooler and more comfortable. But more importantly he developed a new Code of Conduct for more respectability in public places. This Code banned swearing and relaxed the unwritten rules of social etiquette and behavior, allowing the freer mixing of people of different social classes (British Broadcasting Corporation 2014). For the first time this enabled people to network with those of higher social classes, more power and status than themselves – something that was a complete novelty at the time.

Perhaps the most significant legacy that Nash left behind for Bath was his support for, and leadership of, a Georgian building construction boom. He started this off when, in 1708 he ordered the

Assembly Rooms to be built and levied a fee on all visitors to the city. This fee helped raise funds to pay for further civic building work.

In the Assembly Rooms Nash organized dinners, teas, breakfast concerts and balls. As he had cunningly banned all private parties held in peoples' homes such civic social events soon became popular. By 1720, and driven by the ballroom's success, Nash had added a larger ballroom to the Assembly Rooms so that more party-goers could enjoy more, and bigger, parties.

As well as kick-starting Bath's social scene, Nash also played a significant part in civic planning and development. For example he positively encouraged the architect John Wood senior to be employed to design and build what were to become some of Bath's most impressive buildings. These buildings included The Royal Crescent (see Figure 3), King's Circus (now called 'The Circus'), Queen Square and The Royal Mineral Hospital.

Figure 3. The Royal Crescent

ARCHITECTURAL HIGHLIGHTS

If you enjoy 1700s architecture then Bath is the place for you as it was during the 1700s that a lot of Bath's stunning iconic buildings were designed and built. In 1740 the Mineral Water Hospital which was formally known as the Royal National Hospital for Rheumatic Diseases, was built on the corner of what is now Union Street and Upper Borough Walls. Opened in May, 1742 the Mineral Water Hospital was the first hospital in the UK to accept patients from all over the country and so was one of the initial founding blocks of the UK's National Health Service. Nash was instrumental in raising funds to pay for the hospital's construction.

During 1754 the circular King's Circus was completed. The Circus' architect, John Wood senior, may have been inspired by his interest in the ancient structures he saw near Bath, such as the stone circles at Stonehenge and Stanton Drew, as well as in his personal interest in druids and Masonic symbols. Such ancient and mythical symbols can still be seen on the buildings Wood worked on. For example above the first row of pillars built into the façade of The Circus. Also, looking from above, the outline shapes of the Circus and nearby Royal Crescent form the shape of a key. Perhaps this is also a coded message sent to us from the architect? Acorns also perch upon parapets along The Circus which provide other symbolic historical links back to the city's mythical founder Bladud and his pigs.

In the 1760s the same architectural team of John Wood, both senior and younger, was again encouraged by Nash to design and build The Royal Crescent. The Crescent took from 1767 to 1775 to be completed. Around the same time Lord Pulteney was planning a village he named Bathwick, across the river a little way east from Bath where his wife owned an extensive area of land. What they needed to make the village viable however was a bridge across the river to provide easier access to and from Bath city centre. To solve this problem Pulteney employed the architect Robert Adam, to design and eventually build such a bridge in 1770. The bridge was later named Pulteney Bridge in honor its founder. The bridge was designed not just to provide an easy river crossing but, inspired by Florence's Ponte Vecchio, to also house small shops along both sides of the bridge.

Completing the clutch of classical Georgian architectural sites that still exist in Bath, during the 1790s Lansdown Crescent was constructed. This Crescent has many original architectural details still on show such as the original gas street lamps and pleasing fan-shaped doorways. Sometimes sheep are brought in by a local farmer and encouraged to eat the grass at the front of the Crescent. This not only saves on mechanized lawn mowing but also adds some quaint character to the area which also has become an attraction for people wanting to see the sheep in action which is usually during October.

20TH CENTURY BATH

World War Two brought much hardship to the whole country and ruin to many European cities. Although the neighboring industrial city of Bristol was a more important target for enemy bombing raids, Bath did not escape similar violence and destruction. Although Bath wasn't generally a target for German air raids, there was an air raid specifically aimed at Bath during the end of April, 1942 (Created in Bath 2015). The attack came in retaliation for repeated air attacks by the British air force on German targets, the German Luftwaffe decided to send 80 aircraft to bomb historically significant targets in Britain. The sites chosen by the German air commanders were selected using information they found in the German 'Baedeker' travel guides which were popular at the time. Hence the three bombing raids that targeted Bath at this time were nicknamed the 'Baedeker Raids'. Bath wasn't the only target for a Baedeker Raid – the cities of York, Exeter and Norwich were also included. However, back in Bath and on the first night of the raid, the German aircraft arrived at around 11pm, dropping their first load of bombs on the city and its unfortunate surroundings. After returning to base in France and once refueled and reloaded with bombs, the war planes returned at around 4:30am that same night to drop a second barrage of bombs (Daily Mail 2011). During the following night there was yet another bombing raid on Bath which started at around midnight. In total 417 people were killed in Bath even though a lot of the bombs that had been dropped failed to explode due to a miscalculation by the German pilots over the distance the bombs would fall. This error undoubtedly saved lives and a lot of damage to many of the city's buildings.

A memorial to those who died during the raids can be found at the southern entrance to the Royal Victoria Park. Many of the buildings that were damaged have since been restored and so there is little war time destruction now visible in the city.

During 1987 the whole city was awarded United Nations Educational, Scientific and Cultural Organization, (UNESCO) World Heritage status. This provides the people of the city with special powers and responsibilities to preserve its internationally important heritage. As such Bath is a unique and internationally significant place and attracts many visitors throughout the year.

There is also a thriving university just outside the city, and so, especially in term time, students bring an extra buzz. The University has top flight sports facilities and along with the popular Bath Rugby and Cricket Clubs (situated on the eastern side of the river), sports fixtures also play an important part in city life.

2   TRAVEL TO, FROM AND WITHIN BATH

Bath is easy to get to as visitors have a choice of how they wish to arrive: air, rail or road.

AIR

The most convenient airport to Bath is located at Bristol, about 20 miles (32km) away, although Heathrow and Gatwick may provide alternative options for travellers.

BRISTOL AIRPORT

- www.bristolairport.co.uk

The nearest airport is at Bristol which is 20 miles (32km) away. There is a coach service which leaves the airport every 10 minutes and operates every day of the week and throughout the day. The coach takes passengers to Bristol Temple Meads railway station where the journey to Bath can be continued by train. Combined tickets for both the airport coach and the train journey can be purchased from www.trainline.com and the whole journey from the airport to Bath can take as little as an hour.

Heathrow Airport

- www.heathrowairport.com

Britain's busiest airport is undoubtedly Heathrow airport located just west of central London. Heathrow is about 100 miles (160km) east of Bath.

Usefully there is a coach service directly from Heathrow to Bath, operated by National Express, and which takes about 1.5-2 hours depending upon traffic conditions. Another way is to catch the 'Heathrow Express' train from the airport to London Paddington railway station and then a train from Paddington to Bath. This route can take as little as about 1.5 hours.

Gatwick Airport

- www.gatwickairport.com

South of London is Gatwick airport and is a rival to Heathrow as one of Britain's busiest airports. However, as it is about 140 miles (225km) east of Bath, it is also one of the furthest airports for visitors travelling to the Roman spa city. Travellers can take a train from Gatwick to Reading - a city west of London - and hop on a connecting train to Bath. This journey will take at least 3 hours. There is also a coach service run by National Express, from Gatwick airport to Bath which takes about 4.5 hours as it also stops at Heathrow en route.

RAIL

- www.nationalrail.co.uk
- www.thetrainline.co.uk
- www.firstgreatwestern.co.uk

If you are already in Britain, then Bath Spa railway station is easy to travel to by train and is cove ineptly located close to the centre of Bath.

Bath Spa railway station is located on the mainline from London to the west of the country, and so is served by intercity, faster trains, as well as some slower, regional trains. The main services from London depart from Paddington and Waterloo stations, and take about 1.5hrs and 2hrs respectively.

ROAD

The M4 motorway runs horizontally from London towards the west of the country, past the Welsh capital and on towards west Wales. Junction 18 of the M4 is 10 miles (16km) and is the closest to Bath. The M5 motorway which runs roughly north/south up the west side of England intersects the M4 at Bristol, and provides good road access to Devon and Cornwall to the south, and Birmingham and the Lake District to the north.

Park and ride

There are four park-and-ride services in Bath, as well as some limited places for on-street parking. Usually parking charges apply between 8am and 7pm with 'pay and display' car parking ticket machines near the roadside parking spaces. There are 13 city centre car parks with a total of 4000 spaces and split into 'long' or 'short' stay spaces.

As Bath is an older city, there are several one way streets and bus-only lanes throughout the city.

Bicycle

- www.sustrans.org.uk

There are two National Cycle Network routes passing through Bath: Route 4 runs west, using the Bristol-Bath Railway Path and eastwards along the Kennet and Avon canal; Route 24 connects with Route 4 close to Dundas Aqueduct before heading south-west towards the town of Frome.

Within Bath visitors can hire bicycles on a short-term basis. There are several bicycle parking/locking facilities dotted around the city; for example just north of Bath Abbey.

Two Tunnels Greenway

The Two Tunnels route is both a walking- and cycle-path and re-uses what is a disused railway track. This is a dramatic and accessible route leading south from the city - and available for visitors to use on foot, cycle, and wheelchair. The route forms National Cycle Route 24 and joins with National Cycle Route 4 which runs through Bath. The route follows the disused Somerset and Dorset Joint Railway from East Twerton through the Bath suburb of Oldfield Park to the Devonshire Tunnel. It emerges into Lyncombe Vale before entering the Combe Down Tunnel, and then emerges to cross Tucking Mill Viaduct at Tucking Mill and on into the village of Midford (Anonymous 2015). The Devonshire tunnel is a quarter of a mile (400m) in length. Meanwhile, the Combe Down tunnel is just over a mile (1.6km) long and passes under Combe Down. Combe Down tunnel is Britain's longest cycling tunnel (West n.d.). Both tunnels are lit between 5:00am and 11:00pm every day.

Bus

- www.traveline.org.uk
- www.firstgroup.com
- www.bathconnect.com

Bath's bus and coach station is difficult to miss, located in a contemporary rotunda building not far from the railway station.

Being so close to the city centre makes travelling by bus an attractive way to travel around.

3   PLACES OF INTEREST WITHIN THE CITY

AMERICAN MUSEUM

- CLAVERTON MANOR, CLAVERTON, BATH BA2 7BD
- AMERICANMUSEUM.ORG

The American Museum is tucked away about 2.5 miles (4km) outside the centre of Bath south-easterly from the city centre and almost on the top of Claverton Hill. Regardless of this topographical challenge, the museum is still easily accessible by car, bus or by intrepid cyclers and walkers if the, at time steep, ascent is not too off-putting!

Based at Claverton Manor in a house that was built in the 1820s, the Museum is a neighbor of Bath University and the Bath Cats and Dogs home and was founded by American Dallas Pratt and John Judkyn, a Briton – both of whom were keenly interested in antiques. It is located in an area of outstanding natural beauty, and has gorgeous views over the Limpley Stoke Valley and the River Avon. As well as the museum building, 35 acres (14ha) of its grounds and beautiful gardens are also open to visitors.

Focusing upon American cultural history, the American Museum is the only museum of American decorative and folk art outside of the United States of America and has been established since 1961.

The Museum has exhibits describing the history of America including about its indigenous peoples, the first European settlers and through to the twentieth century. As well as permanent exhibitions the museum also has an annually-changing temporary exhibition and American-themed music and 'living history' events.

ASSEMBLY ROOMS

- BENNETT STREET, BATH BA1 2QH
- WWW.BATHVENUES.CO.UK/VENUES/ASSEMBLY-ROOMS

In amongst what seems to be an up-market residential area, the Assembly Rooms can sometimes seem to be a little hidden away. However it is worth the hunt to find them as the Assembly Rooms will reward the determined visitor with glimpses of what life and leisure time was like for Bath's Georgian high society.

In Georgian Britain an Assembly was where people, often of differing social classes and, innovatively for the time both sexes, could freely mix. The Assembly Rooms were contained within one specially-designed building made specifically for Georgian entertainment. Assembly Rooms were typically designed to enable dancing in a Ballroom, gambling in a Card Room and taking, what were then quite fashionable, refreshments in a Tea Room. Assembly Rooms managers often developed the forms of entertainment offered, some holding events such as masked balls, public concerts and more educationally-focused Salons. The Assembly Rooms at

Bath were built for similar purposes and so the building contains a 100 ft (30 m) long Ball Room, an Octagonal Room, a Card Room and a Tea Room. See Figure 4.

The Assembly Rooms were the most fashionable and socially-important meeting place in Bath when it was opened in the 18th century. They were a great place for aristocrats (and other classes) to come to meet, to mingle and to party the night away.

After being bombed during World War Two the building was restored in the 1960s and is now owned by the National Trust. In the Assembly Room's basement is housed a Fashion Museum.

Figure 4. The Tea Room, part of Bath's Assembly Rooms.

BATH ABBEY

- ABBEY CHURCHYARD, BATH BA1 1LT
- WWW.BATHABBEY.ORG

Close to the river and next to the Roman Baths, Bath Abbey is one of the most central and dominant buildings in central Bath. See Figure 2.

Bath Abbey is the stunning medieval church of Saints Peter and Paul and with its magnificent 161ft (49m) high tower, is an easy-to-spot landmark in the centre of the city. Within the tower is the Abbey's peal of 10 bells. Usually flying from a flag pole on the tower is the flag of Saint George, the patron saint of England, with its red cross on a white background. The Abbey's history stretches back to the 750's AD and gained providence when in 973AD, King Edgar was crowned the first king of all England within the Abbey.

Over its history, three different Churches have stood on the site of Bath Abbey. The first was an Anglo-Saxon Abbey Church dating from 757 AD but destroyed by the Norman conquerors of England soon after they arrived in England in 1066. However, about 30 years later, in about 1090, the conquerors set about building a Norman cathedral on the site. As time went on, the Norman building became larger and more costly than the monks in the monastery could afford to maintain and by the end of the 15th century the cathedral was in ruins. Nonetheless, the present Abbey church was founded in

1499, but was razed to the ground during the dissolution of the monasteries in 1539 by order of the then King of England, Henry VIII. However luckily for us now, the Abbey was later rebuilt and reopened in 1611.

From above, the Abbey is cruciform in plan, and seats approximately 1,200 people. It is used for religious services, secular civic ceremonies as well as lectures. The Abbey is a historically-significant and legally protected building and is an active place of worship, with hundreds of congregation members and hundreds of thousands of visitors each year. The Abbey also has within it marvelous fan vaulting which is a great example of a Perpendicular Gothic style church as it also has strong architectural vertical lines, rich and ornate decorations and a single, but unified, open space inside. Along the side of this impressive space are beautiful stained glass windows and some other interesting monuments. The east window depicts scenes from the life of Christ, whilst a similar window in the west side of the Abbey shows scenes from the Old Testament. Similarly interesting is the 'ladder to heaven' on the outside of the church. Angels ascend to heaven - and descend down again a result of the then Bishop of Bath, Oliver King's dream. The Bishop, who had been appointed in 1495, had a dream in which he saw angels ascending and descending a ladder which connected heaven to earth – a vision which he had carved into the façade of the Abbey.

Officially there is no admission charge as the building is a church. However immediately opposite the Abbey entrance and just inside, is a counter selling books with a sign telling of a 'suggested donation', making it difficult to enter without feeling obliged to pay the donation. From its position and signage visitors may automatically presume there is a mandatory entrance charge as it is made to look like that way. Once inside the Abbey, for an additional charge, visitors can take a guided tour of the tower on any day but Sunday. The guided tour takes around an hour and includes standing on top of the Abbey's vaulted ceiling, sitting behind the clock face, seeing the Abbey bells and gaining a birds-eye view out, over the city. However, with 212 steps taking the intrepid to the top of its tower, the tour isn't for everyone. But worry not, as the less energetic visitor to the Abbey is still amply rewarded inside by the peace and tranquillity of this impressive example of Gothic architecture.

BATH ABBEY HERITAGE VAULTS MUSEUM AND CHURCH YARD

- ABBEY CHURCHYARD, BATH BA1 1LT
- WWW.BATHABBEY.ORG

Located on the south side of the Abbey in the restored 18th-century Abbey cellars, this museum focuses upon the development of the Abbey and the buildings that were built on the site before it. Exhibits in the museum include statues and other items, some from Saxon times, and some from the current Abbey. There is also an exhibition that commemorates the history of Christian worship at the Abbey from Roman times to the present day and which offers an insight into the importance of religion in the City's history.

The Abbey churchyard is now a paved area adjacent to the Abbey where you can sometimes listen to buskers and perhaps take some time to rest and relax on a wooden bench, eat an ice cream from a nearby store and 'people watch'. The churchyard is also a popular meeting point for tour groups whether it's a walking tour of the city or visiting the nearby Abbey or Roman Baths. A Visitor Information Centre is also situated here which has an accommodation booking service and information about current events and attractions which visitors may find useful. There are also cafés and other shops nearby as this is a very central location and so is in the very heart of the city.

BATH SPA RAILWAY STATION

- RAILWAY PLACE, BATH, BS1 1SS

Bath railway station is currently the only operational railway station in the city, having been built in 1841. It is located in the southern part of the city at the junction of Dorchester Street and Manvers Street, and on the north bank of the river.

The railway station is now a specially preserved building due to it being a particularly important building of more than special architectural and historical interest. In 2013 it was named as a 'Transport Heritage Site' by the Transport Trust charity (Chronical 2013) with a red circular plaque being installed on the station's wall outside and by the entrance to the ticket office.

The station building was constructed by Isambard Kingdom Brunel who had to carefully minimize the building's impact upon its local environment and so modelled the station on an Elizabethan country house (Heritage 2015) in an effort to blend its architectural character into its surroundings. The station has two storeys made from stone and is Jacobean in style. It has a central upper-storey bay which forms part of a passenger waiting room, the windows of which provide a good view out across the city.

Visitors to Bath travelling by train will find themselves emerging from Bath railway station in a prime position to start exploring the city. After exiting the station on the north-west side, travellers are immediately faced with a number of bars, cafés and restaurants, all based around a central piazza. The piazza and the businesses around it are locally known as the Vaults food quarter and is the result of a regeneration project completed in the early 2000's.

A short walk from the station to the north is the heart of the city. Just beyond the railway station forecourt and the piazza to the west, is Bath's bus and coach station.

BATH BUS AND COACH STATION

- DORCHESTER STREET, BATH

The bus and coach station is a short walk west of Bath railway station and is located in a glass, steel and stone 4-storey rotunda. The rotunda houses the bus operator's offices above the ticket centre at ground level which is clad in glass and stone with a wrap of aluminium tubes, which form a type of veil over the building. The rotunda nicknamed locally as the 'Busometer', is also at one end of a mainly glass enclosed passenger concourse in which passengers can wait for their rides to arrive and depart.

Designed by Wilkinson Eyre, an architects' practice based in London, with 14 bays in which buses and coaches can park, the bus and coach station was completed in 2009 and creates a controversial contrasting architectural style compared to its surroundings.

Botanical Gardens

- Royal Victoria Park, Weston Road, Bath, BA1 2XQ
- www.bathnes.gov.uk/services/sport-leisure-and-parks/parks-opening-times-and-locations/botanic-gardens

A Victorian innovation and a feature within the Royal Victoria Park, the Botanical Gardens was created during 1887 and now covers an area of about 9.5 acres (3.8 hectares). Within the Gardens are various grand trees, shrubs, a herbaceous border, a rock garden with a pool and a collection of heritage shrub roses. Harking back to the city's Roman origins there is also a replica of a Roman Temple which was originally designed to be the City's exhibit at the British Empire Exhibition held in London during 1924.

To mark the Garden's centenary in 1987 the gardens were enlarged to include the Great Dell, which was the site of a disused quarry. This has since been developed into a woodland garden.

Green Park Station

- Green Park Road, Bath BA1 1JB
- www.greenparkstation.co.uk

To the west and a little outside the centre of the city, Green Park Station is situated within an abandoned railway station. Up until the 7th March, 1966 Green Park Station (formerly known as Queen Square Station) was a working railway station. Lying dormant and derelict until the 1980s, the station was refurbished and converted into a space in which local businesses are now successfully trading.

The station still retains the original, vaulted iron and glass station roof and signature Bath stone façade. In the old station buildings is also situated a resident market as well as several different types of markets held on different days of the month. For example, Bath Farmers' market is held every Saturday and an Artisan market is held every second Sunday. There are also independent shops, restaurants and coffee shops, as well as rentable office space for small businesses.

GUILDHALL

- HIGH STREET, BATH BA1 5AW
- WWW.BATHVENUES.CO.UK/VENUES/GUILDHALL

The Guildhall can be seen from, and is just a few steps north of, the Abbey. It was built in 1775 and is now a protected historically-important building. It has a beautiful Bath stone façade which has both attractive supporting columns and decorative detailing. Inside is a banquet hall which is often used for weddings and other special events. The building also continues to house the Register Office, the Mayor's Parlor and the city archives. In these Archives, and by appointment, the Royal Charters (through one of which the Queen granted 'city' status to Bath) can be viewed.

Guildhall Market

- High Street, Bath BA2 4AW
- www.bathguildhallmarket.co.uk

This market is located on the east side of the High Street, between the Guildhall to the south, the Victoria Art Gallery and Bridge Street to the north and New Market Row to the east. Entrances and exits are located on the High Street (next to which is an Art Nouveau 'Market' sign) and New Market Row - directly across the road from the weir in the river Avon, and just down river from, Pulteney Bridge.

There has been a market on this site since the 16th century, although the Guildhall Market began trading during the 1770s. At one time the market had vaults (which still exist), a slaughterhouse and stables (Bath Guildhall Market Traders Association 2015). Nowadays the market houses a variety of stalls including those selling ribbons and wool, to those offering coffee and cake, household items, books and specialty teas.

Herschel Museum of Astronomy

- 19 New King Street, Bath, BA1 2BL
- herschelmuseum.org.uk

Located in the house in which William and his wife, Caroline, Herschel lived between 1777 and 1782, this museum was established on 13th March, 1981 exactly 200 years after Herschel discovered Uranus. The terraced house in which this museum is located is a well-preserved Georgian town house and has five levels. Spread over the five storeys visitors can explore the kitchen, a workshop in which Herschel made telescopes, a gallery, auditorium, and music room. There are also other collections spread around the house and the museum also has various special exhibitions, replica telescopes and astronomical instruments on display, such as celestial and terrestrial globes.

PULTENEY BRIDGE

- PULTENEY BRIDGE, BATH BA2 4AY

As you stroll into Bath from the train station, head along Manvers Street northwards. Once you start to see the Abbey in front of you and towards the north-east, you should also now be able to see one of the prettiest views in Bath, that of the Pulteney Bridge spanning the river Avon. The bridge was named 'Pulteney' after Frances Pulteney who inherited the 1st Earl of Bath's estate on the other side of the river across from the city. Frances was married to William Johnstone who was a Member of Parliament as well as a lawyer. It was William who had the idea to create a new suburb called Bathwick on the family's estate. A bridge was therefore needed to ease transport in to, and out from, the new village to enable Bathwick to prosper.

Pulteney Bridge is one of only four bridges lined with shops in the world. It was designed by Robert Adam in the 1760s and was inspired by the Ponte Vecchio in Florence and Venice's Ponte di Rialto. Adam so planned a Palladian style bridge lined with small shops. Despite concerns that this would prove a bottleneck to traffic (other cities such as London and Bristol had already at that time torn down any buildings still remaining on their bridges), the design was accepted and the bridge built.

Built between 1769 and 1774, Pulteney Bridge was constructed from finely worked limestone ashlar with Welsh slate and lead roofed buildings along its entirety. The bridge is 148ft (45m) long and 58ft (18m) wide. See Figure 5.

The elegance of Adam's original bridge design was short-lived however, as shop owners added extensions, altered windows and raised the roofs. Then in 1800 a storm erupted and the resulting flood damaged the north side so badly that it had to be rebuilt. More alterations followed throughout the 19th century as building owners renovated and remodeled their properties, until in the 20th century concerns began to be raised about the gradual loss of Adam's masterpiece. Such concerns turned to protest, resulting in 1936 the bridge being declared a national monument. The City Council bought out all the shops, and despite interruptions caused by the Second World War, the bridge was fully restored in time for the Festival of Britain in 1951. Nowadays the bridge still has a central roadway with pedestrian footpaths and shops either side.

Figure 5. Pulteney Bridge

Together with the Roman Baths, the Abbey and a couple of other 18th century architectural beauties, Pulteney Bridge belongs to Bath's most popular visitor attractions. Today the bridge is a charming destination, both for the quaint shops that line its interior and for the pretty riverside views of its exterior. This fact is frequently emphasized by the crowd of admirers alongside, and on, Pulteney Bridge.

The river Avon flows under the bridge and there is also an unusual water feature to be seen nearby in the form of a crescent shaped weir that is sometimes used as a testing ground for amateur slaloming canoeists. The weir was built in 1975 to reduce the risk of flooding to central Bath and looks like three mini-waterfalls with water cascading over them. Meanwhile on the south-eastern corner of the bridge, there is a small flight of stone steps leading down below the bridge where there is a café and some shops next to the water, as well as gorgeous views of the bridge architecture. A footpath leads from Pulteney Bridge alongside the river and provides a pedestrian route towards Bath Spa Railway station. About a 10 minute walk from the weir, a narrow stairwell from the riverside footpath leads up and onto the road and pedestrian bridge forming part of North Parade before continuing along the river to the back of Bath Spa railway station. The footpath then continues to follow the river, eventually bringing walkers near to the bus and coach station on Dorchester Street.

PUMP ROOM

- ABBEY CHAMBERS, STALL STREET, BATH BA1 1LZ
- WWW.ROMANBATHS.CO.UK/PUMP-ROOM-RESTAURANT

The Pump Rooms are next to the ancient Roman Baths and just a few steps away from the entrance to Bath Abbey. Built between 1790 and 1795 this neo-classical salon was once the social hub of Bath and is still a place where people come to eat, drink and be entertained. See Figure 6.

Figure 6. Entrances to the Pump Room and Roman Baths.

Visitors to the Pump Rooms can taste Bath's natural spring water as, for over 2,000 years; the idea of the hot spring waters and their possible curative properties has lured visitors. Originally bathing in the waters was <u>the</u> way to be gently restored to health, but in the late 17th century, drinking the waters also became popular.

The water which bubbles up from the ground at Bath fell as rain on the Mendip Hills which lie about 20 miles (32km) south-west from Bath. The water then percolates down through limestone aquifers to a depth of between 1.5 to 3 miles (2 to 4km) where geothermal energy heats the water to between 150 and 200°F (65 to 95°C). Under pressure the heated water rises to ground level along fissures and faults in the limestone, eventually arriving at Bath many years after falling as rain in the Mendips.

In 1983 a new spring-water bore-hole was sunk, providing a clean and safe supply of spa water for drinking in the Pump Room. During prime times, a member of staff wearing an authentically researched costume of 1795 (the year the pump room opened) may offer you a glass of this apparently 'unusual' tasting water. Beware! The water tastes similar to warm seawater and so may not be to everyone's taste. The same hot waters heat the Roman Baths which are next door, as well as provide heating for the Pump Rooms during winter.

The Pump Room Restaurant is a popular place to eat, with contemporary English cuisine on the menu and where sometimes customers are serenaded by the in-house string band the Pump Room Trio, or a solo pianist. There are also a few antiques on display, including a clock presented to the Pump Rooms in 1709.

QUEENS SQUARE

- QUEENS SQUARE, BATH, BA1 2HH

Just a few steps north of the Theatre Royal, Queen Square is the biggest municipal square in Bath. It is relatively easy to identify as in the centre of the Square is an obelisk, also known locally as the Bath Needle. This was erected by Richard Nash to commemorate the visit of the Prince of Wales, and his royal consort during 1738.

Although it is usually quite quiet it is the location of several events throughout the year, including French and Italian markets and an annual French-style boules competition. Jane Austen also stayed at no. 13, Queen Square on one of her visits to Bath. Unfortunately this was one of several houses on the south side of the Square that were destroyed during the 1942 World War II air-raids. The house has however since been restored, along with neighboring buildings, and now forms part of the Francis Hotel.

Roman Baths

- Stall Street, Bath BA1 1LZ
- www.romanbaths.co.uk

Adjacent to Bath Abbey, the Roman Bath's are one of the main tourist attractions in south-west England. At the site visitors can explore the Baths and spa complex which are surprisingly situated below current street level. The buildings above street level date from the 19th century.

At the Roman Baths visitors can experience what the indigenous people, the Celts, and the Romans viewed as a sacred place. The remains of the Roman Temple built in honor of Sulis Minerva can also be seen, as can the Baths themselves and other archeological discoveries from around the site.

There are four main features within the hot spring spa complex: the Sacred Spring; the Roman Temple; the Roman Bath House and a museum which displays Roman artifacts that have been recovered from the site throughout its history. Some of these artifacts were found to have been thrown in the sacred spring, perhaps as religious offerings? The main Bath House also has some Roman soldier statues stood around the side of the Great Bath.

The Romans were lucky to discover the natural spring here as it is the only hot spring water naturally-occurring in the country. The

Romans revered the restorative powers of the mineral-rich waters and loved using the naturally heated water to keep clean and healthy. After finding such a natural resource the Romans quickly developed the hot springs into a spa resort focused upon providing luxurious surroundings where customers could rest and relax. The resort became popular, with people travelling from across the Roman Empire to visit the resort. At the Sacred Spring as it was then called, water at a consistent temperature of 115 °F (46 °C) still rises as it has done for thousands of years.

To the Romans hot springs were mystical phenomena, as they were to the Celts before them. As a result the Romans built a magnificent temple on the site. This temple they dedicated to Sulis Minerva, according to their custom of integrating the worship of local gods, in this case Sulis, with their own deity, Minerva. From this came the Roman name for the city, Aquae Sulis: the waters of Sulis. Harking back to this time, in the Baths museum you can see some of the curses which Romans would etch on pewter discs and throw into the pool to exhort the goddess to punish those they believed had wronged them. Later, in Regency times, bathers would descend to this pool from the Pump Room next door to soak in its mineral-rich water. The Roman temple was constructed in around 60 to 70AD and the bathing complex was gradually built up over the subsequent 300 years.

The Baths have been modified on several occasions, including during the 12th century when John of Tours built a curative bath over the King's spring reservoir and again during the 16th century when the city corporation built a new bath (called the Queen's Bath) to the south of the spring. The centre piece of the complex is the Great Bath itself which the Romans would have used as much more than just a place to bathe. Here they would gather to do business, meet their friends and network. It was a place to see others and to be seen.

The Great Bath is fed with hot water directly from the Sacred Spring and lined with 45 thick sheets of lead. It is about 5ft (1.6m) deep and is accessed by four steep steps that entirely surround it. These steps, the flagged paving around it and the Bath itself, are still intact from Roman times. The tall columns and higher terrace date from the Victorian era when the Baths were rediscovered after centuries left forgotten and lying under the city's streets.

Today, when leaving the baths visitors can go straight into the Pump Room to experience something of the Regency approach to taking the waters.

There is an audio tour guide available for visitors to the Baths. The audio guide commentary has features that complement the main narrative, a separate text for children and additional facts for those who want to learn more about individual areas of the Baths or the items on display. The tour takes in several areas of the Roman Baths and the Regency additions, as well as exhibits on the temple to Sulis Minerva. If the weather conditions are right, visitors can view steam rising from the hot Sacred Spring, as well as the pediment from the Temple in the museum area, and the fridgidarium, where life-size images of Roman bathers are sometimes projected onto the walls.

ROYAL CRESCENT

- ROYAL CRESCENT, BATH BA1 2LR

To the north of Queens Square and little on from the city centre is an up market residential area within which is found the Royal Crescent. See Figure 3. Royal Crescent is one of Bath's best known landmarks, considered to be one of the finest European Crescents still intact, and one of the best examples of Georgian architecture standing anywhere in the UK.

Designed by John Wood junior, the Royal Crescent is a sweep of 30 residential houses, laid out in a crescent shape. The Crescent took from 1767 to 1774 to build with the buildings all looking alike and all made of the locally-favored honey colored Bath stone. In front of the Crescent building there is a long, sloping area of grass separated into two areas: the private lawn of the Crescent and the public grassed area which are separated by a special type of wall called a 'Ha-Ha' wall. A Ha-Ha wall was a common feature of many

17th and 18th century country estates and enabled those looking towards the grounds from the house to have uninterrupted views out across the vista. Meanwhile, the design of the Ha-Ha wall with a sunken stone wall and a deep ditch on the side away from the house meant that it provided an effective barrier to deer, sheep and any other animals, stopping them from being able to enter the more delicate gardens nearer to the house.

The Royal Crescent also includes the Number 1 Royal Crescent Museum and the Royal Crescent Hotel at number 16. The Museum is operated by the Bath Preservation Trust and illustrates how wealthy owners of the period might have furnished and lived in such a house.

The huge curved façade of the Royal Crescent is quite misleading as it appears to comprise of 30 houses, all symmetrically arranged and with their iconic columns standing along the ground floor. However, if viewed from behind the Crescent, this illusion is shattered as varying roof levels and a mix of different decorations are now revealed. These and other architectural additions are the result of each original resident being able to purchase a fixed length of the building and its accompanying façade, with their own specifications then being carried out by their own individual architects. What looks like two houses from the front might actually be the same building. Today most of the houses are privately owned and many of them have been converted into flats. The harmonious frontal appearance has however been retained. The view across Royal Victoria Park makes this one of the most desirable addresses in the city and is one of Bath's unique and 'must see' destinations.

ROYAL VICTORIA PARK

- BOUNDED BY PARK LANE, WESTON ROAD, MARLBOROUGH BUILDINGS AND UPPER BRISTOL ROAD, BATH BA1 2LZ

Located close to Royal Crescent, Royal Victoria Park became a municipal park in 1829 after Bath residents subscribed to protect this green space from being built upon. The typically Victorian style park has been allowed to keep its original features and its charm ever since its creation. It was opened by Princess Victoria who named it 'Royal Victoria Park' – this being an honor for a city park and is, as a result, recognized as a park of national historic importance.

The Park hosts a number of events and concerts throughout the year, as well as having a children's play area and embedded within it, Bath's Botanical Gardens. It also has open spaces and well-maintained planted areas to enjoy. At the south-east entrance is a plaque and statue in memory to the Park's royal patron, Queen Victoria.

THE HOLBOURNE MUSEUM AND SYDNEY GARDENS

- GREAT PULTENEY STREET, BATH BA2 4DB
- WWW.HOLBURNE.ORG

Travel from west to east along Pulteney Bridge, keep going straight along Argyle Street and then along Great Pulteney Street and visitors will eventually come to the Holbourne Museum standing at one entrance to Sydney Gardens. The Museum's collection of interesting and significant artwork was created by the late Sir William Holburne, the fifth Baronet of Menstrie who lived between 1793 and 1874. Sir William inherited his fortune and so was able to forgo a military career, instead spending time travelling around Europe building-up his art collection.

As visitors approach the Museum, they will see that it is housed in a grand Georgian looking building with pretty gardens surrounding it. With an impressive entrance, visitors who take the time to walk around the building might be surprised to find a contemporary extension to the building at its rear. This part of the building now houses a pleasant, glass-walled café with great views out, across the Garden and beyond.

The Museum houses a collection of British paintings with several artists such as Gainsborough and Thomas Barker who resided in Bath during the Georgian period. The collection also includes examples of fine china, silver and textiles. The Museum also has temporary exhibitions as well as regularly hosting lectures, concerts and other events.

Technological development in transport brought firstly the canal, and then the railway to Bath. The canal goes past Sydney Gardens to the east, whilst the railway line goes underneath and through part of the Garden. This may seem sacrilegious to some, but the railway lines are submerged within the Garden, with interesting footbridges allowing those enjoying the Gardens unhindered passage across the tracks. Although not the largest of gardens, these grounds do enable visitors to relax surrounded by neatly kept lawns and some magnificent old trees. There are also some interesting buildings within the grounds.

THE CIRCUS

- THE CIRCUS, BATH BA1 2EW

Eastwards along from the Royal Crescent, the Circus has nothing to do with clowns and lion tamers. 'Circus' is the Latin word for circle and the Circus here is a circle of three large buildings designed by one of Bath's main architects, John Wood the Elder. The elder Wood died before it was completed so his son John Wood the Younger completed the project.

Another magnificent example of Georgian architecture, the 33 houses comprising the Circus form a perfect circle with the three streets entering each arranged at a 120° angle to each other. This does not only make sure that the buildings' façades are easily seen when entering the Circus but also gives rise to sumptuous symmetry.

Many elements from classic Roman architecture were used in these buildings. The design of the Circus may have actually been inspired by the Roman Coliseum. The buildings' façades, made from Bath stone, include exquisite details such as triglyphs and mythical and historical emblems. Decorations such as acorns on the top of the houses were also designed to honor King Bladud who, according to legend, founded the city of Bath. But perhaps the most interesting decorations on the buildings are the more than 500 symbols found carved into the frieze. Perhaps these form a mysterious kind of coded message left by the architect?

In the middle of the Circus is a tree planted garden which only adds to the whole aesthetic appeal of the place. Wood's initial plan for the central part of the Circus was thought to be something like a stage for sports and musical events and other gladiatorial–like performances.

THEATRE ROYAL

- Saw Close, Bath BA1 1ET
- www.theatreroyal.org.uk

West from the Roman Baths and south from the Circus, the Theatre Royal is a popular place of entertainment. It has a famous and busy schedule of performances appearing throughout the year.

During 1768 a special Act of Parliament granted a Royal Patent to the theatre which turned it into a 'Theatre Royal', and the first Theatre Royal to be created outside London. As a result the Theatre's reputation grew and a season in Bath was as important for actors as a London billing.

The present theatre building is another great example of Georgian architecture and is also legally protected due to its architectural and historical importance. Rebuilt on its current site a year after a fire in 1882, the theatre now has three auditoria: the Main House, Ustinov Studio and the Egg Theatre. Inside the theatre is a pretty trompe-l'œil ceiling and an ornate, suspended chandelier.

A small plaque on the outside of the southern wall of the Theatre signifies that the present entrance to the Theatre Royal was once part of Beau Nash's first house. Nash's second house is still standing just across the road from the Theatre entrance to the north.

Thermae Bath Spa

- Hot Bath Street, Bath BA1 1SJ
- www.thermaebathspa.com

Open to the public since August 2006, Thermae Bath Spa is a place for people to rest and relax. Not to be confused with the 2000 year old Roman Baths not far away to the east, the Thermae Bath Spa is a modern Spa Centre which is also fed by Bath's natural hot spring water.

Possibly the best part of the modern Spa experience is enjoying the open-air (but heated) roof-top swimming pool. Here swimmers can gently exercise whilst soaking-in views from out and across the city's rooftops which is truly a unique view. Other offerings available at the spa complex include mud wraps, massaging water jets and other hydroponic delights. There is also a visitor centre which enables visitors to learn about the historic development of the Spa from Roman times to the present day.

Victoria Art Gallery

Bridge Street, Bath, BA2 4AT
www.victoriagal.org.uk/

Not far from Pulteney Bridge, and operated by the local government, Victoria Art Gallery is a public art museum. Situated within a specially preserved building that was designed in 1897, the

Gallery was named to celebrate Queen Victoria's sixtieth year as Queen (Council 2015). On the exterior of the building are friezes of classical figures and a statue of Queen Victoria.

Although not a large Art Gallery, the bulk of it is free for visitors to look around, although there are charges for some special, and temporary, exhibitions. The Gallery contains work from Edwardian, Georgian and Victorian periods, as well as the late 20th century. Inside the building visitors will find four galleries housing current displays and exhibitions, along with a shop. The main gallery houses ceramics, glassware, paintings and other art pieces. There is also plenty of seating areas and an area for children.

4   Around Bath and further afield

Bristol

Bristol is Bath's westerly neighbour, being only 15 miles (24km) away and an easy cycle ride, or about 40 minutes by car and 15 minutes by train, ride away.

Like Bath, Bristol has a rich historical heritage, with its wealth being built upon the slave trade with the merchants who plied that trade building their homes in Bristol. However, without the significant .Georgian developments that Bath has, Bristol has a much different look to it. It is also bigger and much more spread out geographically. Bristol also has two Universities within the city: the University of Bristol and the University of the West of England. These attract a large number of students each year and so some parts of Bristol have a lot of buzzing energy which has driven the development of much of the city.

At the heart of the city is the harbour side development which is based upon the old harbour where exports were brought in on ships for unloading. Now the harbour side still retains its historical links, with an industrial museum on the south side of the docks. All around the other sides of the docks is a mixture of upmarket apartments and waterside housing, lots of bars, cafes and restaurants too. At its westerly edge, the harbour links to the river Avon, which flows under Clifton suspension bridge. This bridge was built by Isambard Kingdom Brunel as part of his transport link from London to North America. The bridge is still operational and can be used to travel from the posh Clifton area of Bristol over the river towards the Ashton Court Estate.

CARDIFF

Cardiff was once the throbbing center of the powerful international coal trade and is now the thriving cosmopolitan shopping, eating and sightseeing center of south Wales.

Cardiff is located about 56 miles (90km) west of Bath about one hour by direct train. The capital of Wales, Cardiff is home to around 600,000 people and has a rich industrial heritage. In the 1700 and 1800s, iron and coal were extensively mined from an area called the Welsh Valleys, situated just north of Cardiff. These resources were sold abroad and exported via rail and ships which would be loaded when moored in the docks at Cardiff Bay. Now the coal has stopped being mined, Cardiff Bay has been redeveloped into a beautiful waterside area, and is the home to the Welsh government. The Bay has a circular 6 mile (10km) pedestrianised route around it, as well as visitor attractions such as the world renowned Dr Who experience, a Norwegian Church, the Millennium Centre which hosts theatre and musical shows, a bird life reserve, a five star hotel and is home to a BBC film studio.

As well as Cardiff Bay, the city centre of Cardiff, about 0.5miles to the north of Cardiff Bay, has a large, two storey modern shopping mall, several older but well kept Victorian malls and various independent stores, bars, cafes and restaurants.

Cardiff is also the home of the Welsh rugby team at the iconic Welsh Millennium Stadium which is nearby Cardiff castle, behind which is a beautiful arboretum and civic centre.

Cardiff Bay is the powerful epicenter of the Welsh government and a magnificent go-to place for fun and excitement. If, after all that, you still have energy, then take a trip out of Cardiff to the nearby towns of Penarth - with it's gorgeous and restored pier and esplanade, or Cowbridge - with its green and harmonious Physic Garden and buzzing cafe culture.

KENNET AND AVON CANAL

The Kennet and Avon canal is more than its name implies as it actually comprises of two navigable rivers connected by a canal and is 87 miles (140km) long in its entirety. At its eastern end, the river Kennet joins the river Thames at Reading and is connected to the canal further west at Newbury. The canal then runs westward to Hungerford, along the Vale of Pewsey, through Bradford-on-Avon and on to Bath. In the centre of Bath the canal connects to the River Avon which then flows through Bristol and on to the Severn estuary via Avonmouth.

The canal section was built around 1800 but soon started to fall into disrepair once the Great Western Railway was opened in the 1830s and the faster railway sucked the trade away from the slower canal. However during the 1970s and 1980s the canal was restored and is now a popular visitor attraction for those who enjoy spending time exploring this part of Britain's waterways. The canal and river provide great opportunities for walks or cycle rides along the tow path or trips on pleasure boats of different kinds, from canoes to day cruises. For example, those walking or cycling approximately 2.5 miles (4km) eastward from Bath, along the canal footpath to Bathampton will find a pleasant canal-side spot to refresh, rest and recover before returning.

The route is well-surfaced and is good for anything from a short walk with friends, to a 13 mile largely traffic free 'Bath Half Marathon' circular route out to Dundas Aqueduct, and then back via the canal towpath.

LONDON

London is east of Bath, about 116 miles (187km) away. However with direct coach and train services running from Bath to London, it is easy for those visiting Bath to get to, even for a day trip. The journey from Bath to London takes around 3 hours by car and about 2 hours by train. However, being the capital on Britain, and with around 6 million inhabitants, London has a lot to see and do and really needs much more than a day to explore.

A lot of the key attractions can be found in the centre of London, although visitors may also like to explore further afield, especially if they have a specific interest or attraction in mind to visit. However London probably has something for everyone, whether you enjoy history, food, shopping, art, music and culture.

Arriving from Bath on the train, visitors will arrive at Paddington Station, and by bus at Victoria coach station. By then using the London Underground or over ground public transport system, travellers can easily move around the city.

As with most capital cities, London can seem a busy place and so booking ahead is recommended, especially if accommodation is required. The morning and late afternoon/early evening rush hours can sometimes mean public transport is busy and so to get the most from your journey, it may be a good idea to try to avoid travelling during those times.

OXFORD

Probably most famous for its old university, Oxford is a quaint and charming city some 82 miles (132km) from Bath.

Visitors to Oxford may already be familiar with this historical University city. With Oxford University being one of the oldest universities in the world, many visitors come here to admire its heritage and ancient architecture. With such important buildings and the large number of visitors they attract, Oxford has managed to retain its importance as a working city at the forefront of science, research and learning. It is a beautiful city. Visitors can climb some of the spires dotted throughout the city and revel in the cityscape from such an amazing vantage point. Oxford also has the expected shopping facilities one would expect from a university town - as well as student-friendly bars, cafes and restaurants, sports and other academic events and facilities.

Oxford too has a river pin which visitors can enjoy boat trips, or perhaps walk along its banks.

STONEHENGE

The world famous stone circle that forms part of Stonehenge is 33miles (55km) south-east from Bath which should take about 1 hour by car. This prehistoric monument and burial mound is located in the county of Wiltshire and is thought to have been built around 2500BC. Like Bath, Stonehenge is a UNESCO World Heritage site and a must-see destination for history buffs.

THE COTSWOLDS

The Cotswolds is an area of outstanding natural beauty in southern England located between Bath, Cheltenham, Oxford and Stratford-upon-Avon. With many stunning historic buildings, gardens, nature reserves and the remains of Roman buildings, visitors will be spellbound by the area's quaint charm and amazing beauty. Although served by some public transport, it's much more convenient to traverse the Cotswolds by car if possible as some of the smaller towns and villages may be difficult to get to via public transport. In this way visitors can enjoy the stunning scenery whilst visiting cute and strange-sounding towns and villages such as Winchcombe, Broadway and the Slaughters.

5   Suggested itineraries

It would be very difficult to fit everything that Bath has to offer into half a day. Indeed to do Bath full justice, 2 to 3 days at least would be needed. This would give you more time to fully explore some of the city and its attractions, and you'd leave with a sweet yearning to return to complete your exploration.

Arriving, perhaps by train at the historically important Bath Spa railway station or by coach at Bath's 'Busometer' bus and coach station, you'd quickly be able to feast your eyes upon Bath's treasures. Alternatively you might prefer to drive into this city and park-up in one of the very central car parks. Regardless of how you get here, central Bath is relatively compact and so enables visitors to gain a lot of enjoyment in a relatively small area.

In this chapter are four suggestions for themed self-guided walking tours around the city which are all designed for newcomers to Bath who have may be a half day or, if at a slower pace, a full day in which to explore. The itineraries shown below don't consider refreshment breaks, as everyone has different needs, likes and dislikes. However, being within a cosmopolitan city, there are lots of opportunities for those on these tours to stop for a while to refuel and rest.

The first suggestion is a 'See all the sights', aimed at those who want to experience all the key tourist attractions within the heart of the city. The next is entitled 'Living history: A Roman and Georgian Jewel' which focuses upon the historically important areas of Bath. The Parks and Gardens themed walk is for those who want to experience quieter and greener places within the city, and perhaps is ideal for those wanting to take a picnic on a fine day. The Museums tour provides visitors insight into how the city and its people developed with respect to its homes, religion, science and fashion. Finally, although not strictly a tour, some suggestions as to the best areas for shopping are also provided at the end of the chapter.

See all the sights

Bath Abbey > Pump Rooms > Roman Baths > Theatre Royal > Queens Square > Jane Austin Centre > The Circus > Royal Crescent > Victoria Park > Botanical Gardens > Milsom Street > New Bond Street > Pulteney Bridge > Bath Abbey

If you enjoy walking then this tour is for you! Starting at the Abbey, during this walk you'll learn about ancient beliefs and theatre royalty. Moving on and enjoying Georgian gorgeousness as you go, this stroll also takes you into a Royal park. If time, energy and finances allow, pause for some super shopping before returning to the Abbey via the quaint and historically interesting, Pulteney Bridge.

A short distance of about 530yds (500m) north from the train and bus stations is the easy-to-find Bath Abbey. It's hard to miss the Abbey due to its impressive tower which is a famous landmark amongst the central Bath skyline. This is the perfect place to start your walking tour of Bath and get a sense of the historical importance of the place and the lie of the land. As you look around inside the Abbey, you may like to climb the steps up to the top of its tower to enjoy unparalleled views across the city and literally to look forward to what else you have to explore.

This walk could take as little as an hour or two if walkers didn't spend much time at each point of interest. A more relaxing day could easily be spent on enjoying this walk, especially if time was taken along the way to stop and explore, and take on board refreshments. The train station and the centre of the city are built on low ground not far from the river. This means that there is a slope upwards towards Royal Crescent and the hills beyond. The total distance of this walk is approximately 2.5 miles (4km) without considering walking around any of the places of interest. Please note though that Bath is a hilly city and this walk requires a gentle climb as you move up from the Abbey to the Royal Crescent.

A few steps west from the Abbey entrance are the Pump Rooms where residents used to come and dance and socialise. May be more famously, here too are the old Roman Baths – an example of one of the best preserved ancient spas in the world.

After exploring the spa and turning north out of the Baths and then west along Westgate Street brings you to the Theatre Royal. This splendid old theatre still hosts plays and shows. You never know, if you keep alert you may spot a celebrity in a nearby café. On northwards from the theatre brings you alongside Queen Square. This Square is surrounded by Georgian Houses and was one of the first examples of Georgian domestic architecture. The construction of the houses was funded by Beau Nash and they were designed to look like one, large mansion house when viewed from the south. The obelisk in the middle of the Square commemorates the visit of Frederick, Prince of Wales in 1738.

About 350yds (320m) north from Queen Square, along Gay Street, brings you to The Circus after passing-by the Jane Austin Centre (an ideal stopping point for fans of the author) near the junction of Gay Street and Old King Street. Upon leaving The Circus, and heading west along Brock Street, you come to the Royal Crescent which rewards visitors with amazing views of probably Bath's finest Georgian architecture.

If time allows, head westward again and 0.4 miles (650m) from Royal Crescent, is Royal Victoria Park which has within it a 9.5 acre (3.8ha) Botanical Garden. Returning back now eastwards through the park along Royal Avenue will allow you to pass along Queens Parade Place and on to George Street. This allows you to move southwards towards, and then into, the shopping area of Milsom and New Bond Streets before continuing south along New Bond Street Place. Appearing at Upper Borough Walls, you'd be wise to head east towards Northgate Street. Keep moving eastwards and head for Bridge Street and you'll see Pulteney Bridge appear in front of you. It's then just a 0.2 mile (330m) stroll south along Grand Parade to your starting point at Bath Abbey.

LIVING HISTORY: A ROMAN AND GEORGIAN JEWEL

Bath Abbey > Abbey Vaults Museum > Roman Baths > Pump Rooms > Mineral Hospital > city walls > Theatre Royal > Queens Square > Royal Crescent > The Circus > Assembly Rooms > Pulteney Bridge > Guildhall Market > Bath Abbey

For history buffs, especially those interested in Roman, and especially Georgian relics and architecture, Bath is a 'must see' destination. There are not so many places in the UK that have so many historical assets which have been preserved so well, and which are found so close together.

Of course the Roman baths and the Abbey provide easy-to-find and an obvious starting point for any historical tour. Being one of the best preserved examples of Roman heritage it would almost be a crime not to visit them! After taking the spa waters, travellers on this tour can move forward in time to the 1700s. With a clear linage which started with the forward-thinking Beau Nash, Bath's Georgian heritage is one of the most outstanding locations for its well preserved and stunningly beautiful architecture.

Here is a suggestion for a walking tour that takes in both the Roman as well as the Georgian marvels that Bath has to offer. If visitors wish to linger at each place of interest, the tour will take longer than suggested. Also no account has been taken for refreshment breaks. However all the sites mentioned on this tour are within, or very nearby, the city centre and the many cafes, bars and restaurants found within.

Starting at the Bath Abbey, visitors can first explore inside this church, not forgetting the museum in its vaults. Just opposite the main entrance to the Abbey are the Roman Baths and the Pump Rooms which are a 'must see' on any ones Bath itinerary. The Mineral hospital was one of the foundations of Britain's National Health Service and can still be seen not far from the Pump Rooms to the north. Walking past the Mineral Hospital and visitors will come to remnants of the old city walls. Further along the road to the west is the Theatre Royal which hosts shows in a building not far from the Georgian VIP Richard Nash's home. Moving on, northwards from the theatre, Queens Square and its central obelisk are next. Just on from the Square's north east corner, visitors can experience the Royal Crescent via a World War Two memorial. Moving out of the Royal Crescent, along Brock Street, is The Circus, an interesting an ornately decorated circle of Georgian homes. A short stroll along Bennett Street a visit to the Assembly Rooms can be enjoyed before moving on to Pulteney Bridge. From Pulteney Bridge visitors can walk through Guildhall Market, emerging on the other side and within clear view once again of Bath Abbey, just to the south of the marker entrance/exit.

PARKS AND GARDENS - GREEN, OPEN SPACES

Victoria Park and Botanical Gardens > Royal Crescent lawn and Ha-Ha wall > Green space centre of the Circus > Sydney Gardens > The Parade Gardens

If green spaces are your idea of relaxing places, then Bath is a good place for you. Within short distance from the centre of the city are several parks and gardens open to the public to enjoy. One of the biggest is Victoria Park and the Botanical Gardens situated within it. This was designated a 'Royal Park' and as such has special historical interest and links to Queen Victoria whom it honours. Nearby is the Royal Crescent with its large and open green lawn which sweeps down, southwards from the buildings that make up the Royal Crescent. For garden buffs, this large lawn has a 'ha-ha' wall running east-west across. The wall is a nod of recognition to similar walls used by estate owners to ensure that their livestock were kept away from near to the house. After the Royal Crescent a quick visit to the Circus rewards visitors with the circular green space at the heart of this round row of Georgian houses. Moving on towards Pulteney Bridge brings visitors a choice: either go towards Holbourne House and explore Sydney Gardens at its rear; or venture southwards along the riverbank, on the west side of which are the Parade Gardens for which an admission fee is charged.

MUSEUMS – A LOOK AT TIMES GONE BY

Bath Abbey Vaults > Roman Baths > No 1 Royal Crescent museum > Herschel museum > Fashion museum in the Assembly Rooms > if time allows, the American Museum

As befits a city containing numerous buildings of historical importance, Bath has several outstanding museums where visitors can learn about significant events in the city's history.

Starting at the Bath Abbey Vaults, visitors can experience this historic Abbey church building as well as learn about its beginnings and subsequent development. Just around the corner are the world-famous Roman Baths, a splendid example of a Roman spa resort. William Herschel, he who discovered Jupiter and a master telescope maker is remember at the Herschel Museum located in Herschel's former home. Moving northwards, the Number One Royal Crescent Museum provides visitors the opportunity to experience a fine Georgian home. The Fashion Museum, housed in the basement of the Assembly Rooms would bring visitors back towards the city centre and provide the chance to discover how fashion has changed through the ages.

If time and stamina allows, visitors could catch a bus up to the American Museum which is about a 20 minute bus journey out of the city towards the University of Bath.

SHOPPING

Southgate Shopping Centre > Southgate Street > Stall Street > Union Street > Along and off the sides of Milsom Street > Bartlett Street Quarter > Broad Street > Pulteney Bridge

Bath is a shopper's paradise as it has a wide range of shops of all types and sizes. Although not really a tour as such, shopping is the focus of many visitors' trips to Bath and so this mini guide to the shopping hotspots within the city centre is included below.

There are many traditional and popular chain-stores and department stores which visitors to other British towns and cities will be familiar with. There are also numerous independent businesses situated within Bath, as well as market stalls, cafés and restaurants. If markets are more interesting to you, Green Park Station and the Guildhall Markets are good places to aim for.

Nearest to Bath Spa railway station and just to the north, is the Southgate Shopping Centre which is a pedestrians-only area of concentrated shopping opportunities. Shops stocking major branded goods are located within this retail zone.

Moving north up Southgate Street and then continuing along Stall Street and then Union Street, shoppers will discover an array of interesting independent, as well as some other well-known shops. At the northern end of Union Street are the Upper Borough Walls –

a street orientated east-west. North of this are several smaller streets, such as Burton Street, which also have smaller shops along them. At the north end of Burton Street is Milsom Street, which tends to have higher-end shops and fine dining restaurants and cafés dotted along it as well as just off it to either side.

At the northern extremity of the main shopping area, and a short walk from the northern end of Milsom Street, easterly along George Street, is the Bartlett Street Quarter. This short street is packed with high-end boutiques, cafés and restaurants, and is a good place to pause and have some refreshment.

Coming south and down the hill from Bartlett Street Quarter, shoppers could head south down Broad Street towards Pulteney Bridge. Broad Street is also full of interesting shops, as are Saracen and Walcot Streets – plus both are on the way to the older shops situated upon Pulteney Bridge.

Around Bath Abbey are typical tourist-focussed shops selling souvenirs, postcards and the like to those hunting for gifts for loved ones or a memento for themselves. Also near the Abbey are several cafés, ice-cream and snack bars and restaurants.

6 WORKS CITED

Anonymous. *Two Tunnels Greenway.* 2015. https://en.wikipedia.org/wiki/Two_Tunnels_Greenway (accessed September 22, 2015).

Bath and North East Somerset Local Authority. "Bath City-wide Character Appraisal." *Bath City-Wide Character Appraisal SPD.* Bath and North East Somerset Local Authority. 31 August 2005. http://www.bathnes.gov.uk/sites/default/files/sitedocuments/Planning-and-Building-Control/Planning-Policy/SPDs/bath_city-wide_character_appraisal_spd.pdf (accessed July 2, 2015).

Bath Guildhall Market Traders Association. *About.* 2015. http://www.bathguildhallmarket.co.uk/about/ (accessed July 3, 2015).

British Broadcasting Corporation. *Local legends - Beua Nash's Bath.* 18 June 2014. http://www.bbc.co.uk/legacies/myths_legends/england/somerset/article_4.shtml (accessed April 9, 2015).

Chronical, Bath. *Brunel's Bath Spa Railways Station named as Transport Heritage Site.* 2013. http://www.bathchronicle.co.uk/Brunel-s-Bath-Spa-Railways-

Station-named/story-18210407-detail/story.html (accessed September 22, 2015).

Council, Bath and North Easte Somerset. *Victoria Art Gallery - About.* 2015. http://www.victoriagal.org.uk/about (accessed September 22, 2015).

Created in Bath. *World War 2.* 24 April 2015. http://www.bath.co.uk/history/bath-through-the-ages-world-war-2 (accessed April 24, 2015).

Daily Mail. *The forgotten Blitz: When Hitler sent the Luftwaffe to bomb our most beautiful cities, Bath was hit hard - now survivors reveal all in a new documentary.* 5 August 2011. http://www.dailymail.co.uk/femail/article-2022809/The-forgotten-Blitz-When-Hitler-sent-Luftwaffe-bomb-beautiful-cities-Bath-hit-hard--survivors-reveal-new-documentary.html (accessed April 24, 2015).

Heritage, Our Transport. *Heritage Locations - Bath Spa Station and railway approaches.* 2015. http://transportheritage.com/find-heritage-locations.html?sobi2Task=sobi2Details&sobi2Id=712 (accessed September 22, 2015).

Mayor of Bath. *Royal Charters.* 2015. http://www.mayorofbath.co.uk/royal-charters (accessed April 9, 2015).

Smith, R. *World Heritage Sites of Britain: a guide to all of Britain's world-class places of interest.* Basingstoke: AA Publishing, 2010.

United Nations Education, Scientific and Cultural Organization. *City of Bath.* 2015. http://whc.unesco.org/en/list/428 (accessed April 8, 2015).

University of Bath. *Home page.* 2015. http://www.bath.ac.uk/ (accessed April 9, 2015).

West, Outdoors. *The Two Tunnels Greenway, Bath.* http://www.outdoorswest.org.uk/Home/maps-and-routes/the-two-tunnels-greenway-bath (accessed September 22, 2015).

Printed in Great Britain
by Amazon